FALMOUTH BAY UNDERWATER

A GUIDE TO SOME OF THE

WRECKS,

MARINE LIFE,

AS WELL AS SNORKELLING AND

SCUBA DIVING SITES AROUND

FALMOUTH

BY

MARK MILBURN

Copyright © 2017 Mark Milburn
All rights reserved.
ISBN: 9781549830044

PREFACE

Mark Milburn originally created a series of mini guides, to try to help promote Falmouth as a diving location. The original guides have now been largely rewritten and collated, into this more complete guide. Falmouth has been a popular diving location for decades, but, ever since the Scylla was sunk as an artificial reef in Whitsand Bay, too many divers have forgotten about Falmouth. The original series of guides were quite basic and without too many photos. This book expands on that concept, to create a useful guide to Falmouth Underwater.

Mark Milburn is an S.D.I. (Scuba Diving International) and T.D.I. (Technical Diving International) Instructor. Teaching people to dive and a wide range of further education 'diving speciality' courses, from his dive centre near Falmouth, diving for pleasure when he can. He is also qualified on several scuba diving closed circuit rebreathers (CCR), as well as mixed gases, for deep diving down to 100m. He is also a qualified AIDA freediver. He owns and operates two Rigid Hulled Inflatable Boats, both are fitted out with some of the latest technology for underwater surveying and hunting wrecks, including side scan sonar and magnetometers.

Over the years he has written published articles and press releases for several online websites, as well as in some of the U.K. national dive magazines. With over two thousand dives completed in and around Falmouth Bay, he knows the area quite well, he says "I spend more time underwater than I do at home".

Reef Scene

Contents

Acknowledgments	Page 06
Wrecks	Page 07
Marine Life	Page 21
Snorkelling and Shore Diving	Page 64
Reef Dives	Page 80
Wreck Dives	Page 90
Manacles	Page 100
Glossary	Page 108
Bibliography	Page 110
Further Reading	Page 111

ACKNOWLEDGMENTS

Mark would like to thank the following for their help and advice over the years:

Kevin Heath

John Elliss

Nick Lyon

Kirstie Harris

Paul Harry - Aeroworks AVS

Ruth Holding

Peter Holt

Alison James

Serena Cant

Shaun Beedie

Historic England

Falmouth Bay's Wrecks

A Mixed Bag

Wars and Winds

Falmouth has been an important Cornish port since before records even began. It is the largest port in Cornwall and because of it's unique position, it is probably one of the most sheltered ports in Cornwall. The winds have still taken their toll, in and around the port, especially in the age of sail. Whereas war caused the most casualties during the age of steam. Navigational errors have caused a lot of the wrecks on the Manacles, an exposed reef system that has taken around fifty known vessels over the years. This section will look at a few of the more well known wrecks within the Falmouth Bay area. Starting with the shallowest wreck first, then getting deeper as we go. This section is not a dive guide, there are diving guide sections later in this book, this is just a little history of some of the wrecks. It is a real 'mixed bag' of wrecks.

Falmouth sea front, Pendennis headland and the Carrick Roads behind

The shallowest ship wreck still visible around Falmouth Bay, is the Ben Asdale. This four hundred and twenty two ton fishing trawler came to grief in December 1978, when it's hydraulic steering completely failed. It's anchors dragged and it was then blown ashore, onto the rocks close to Maenporth Beach. At low water spring tides you can walk around the remains of the Ben Asdale. Even though it is a relatively young wreck, it is now very broken after being partially salvaged, a few times. There are a couple of large deck winches visible, lying within the remains. The ships eight cylinder diesel engine and some pieces of it's superstructure also remain, as shown in the second and third photo below. The remains can be viewed from above quite easily, from an area close to the coastal path. There is a narrow side track from the coastal path, where you get almost above the wreck. It is a steep cliff edge, so do take care if you go there. The following two images were taken from that location.

At sometime during 2016, another piece of wreckage had been removed. A large brass item looked like it had been cut off with a large angle grinder.

The 422 ton fishing trawler, the Ben Asdale soon after the wrecking

The Ben Asdale today

The Ben Asdale on a low spring tide

Next on the list are the remains of UB-86, a German WWI U-Boat. It is another wreck that breaks the surface at low water but only by about half a meter. At the end of WWI the Keiser's High Seas fleet scuttled itself at Scapa Flow, the surrendered U-boats went to Harwich. Most of the submarines were distributed around the various naval depots in the U.K., as part of the war reparations scheme. The actual number of U-Boats dispatched to Falmouth must be known somewhere, but, the available records varies, from between five to nine vessels. One or maybe two of the U-Boats were sunk as target practice by the navy, the remaining submarines were then moored up in the bay. They were to be used in explosive trials to find their weaknesses. After the trials were finished, they were hauled up onto the rocks. There is rumour of a terrific storm that wrecked the submarines, that may be why they were left without further trials. One of UB-86's ribs, with some plating attached, can be seen sticking out of the water off Pendennis Point, on a low spring tide. On the lowest of tides there is quite a lot exposed at the surface.

Part of UB-86 protruding from the water on a low tide.

Close to UB-86, are the remains of UB-112, it is impossible to identify these submarines now, as they have been heavily salvaged over the years. Photographs taken close to the time of wrecking identified both UB-86 and UB-112. The only other major submarine remains are of UC-92 just off Castle Beach. An unconfirmed story states that the submarine was dragged up the beach at high tide, to be salvaged, official records say that it was lifted and scrapped, which is obviously not correct. Again, it has been heavily salvaged, approximately only the lower twenty five percent remain. The top of the submarine's wreckage, stands proud of the water roughly 0.3m on a low spring tide. This wreck was identified by a survey, completed by Wessex Archaeology during 2013.

Part of the remains of UC-92 sticking out of the water on a low spring tide at Castle Beach, this was close to the bow, it is the location of the six one metre diameter shafts that held the mines.

During November 1916, the 5077 ton British Cargo Steamer, the s.s. Ponus, came ashore near Gyllyngvase Beach. It was built in 1902 as an oil tanker by Russell & Co., Port Glasgow. After being driven up onto the rocks it caught fire, it then kept Falmouth lit for three days and three nights. A storm in 1917 broke the ship into two pieces with a large gap between them, the remaining standing sections were salvaged, leaving behind the flattened remains of the middle section. The ship's remains are now spread over a large area.

Oil painting looking at the s.s. Ponus on fire, from Swanpool Beach

ss Ponus today. The straight line off the end of the reef

HMS Torrid (F80) was an R Class Destroyer en-route to the breakers yard in 1937. It was anchored in the Carrick Roads in a south easterly gale, when she dragged anchors and was driven high up onto the rocks at Trefusis Point. It stayed there for three years before being salvaged, very little of it remains in around 6m of water.

Trefusis Point behind Falmouth Docks, with Mylor Harbour behind far left.

Almost next to the remains of the Torrid lies what is left of the British sailing ship, the Queen. The Queen transport ship was lost during a south easterly gale in 1814, while sheltering in the Carrick Roads. It had been moored there for three days, seeking shelter after a rough crossing from Portugal. It was carrying wounded troops from Wellington's army, women, children and French prisoners. Its single mooring anchor gave way and she was dashed onto the rocks, three hundred and sixty nine souls perished.

There is a mass grave for the victims in Mylor Churchyard with a single grave stone, dedicated :-

"To the Memory of the Warriors, Women and Children, who on their return to England from the Coast of Spain; unhappily perished in the Wreck of the Queen Transport, on Trefusis Point, Jan 14, 1814.

This stone is erected as a Testimony of regret for their fate by the Inhabitants oft this Parish."

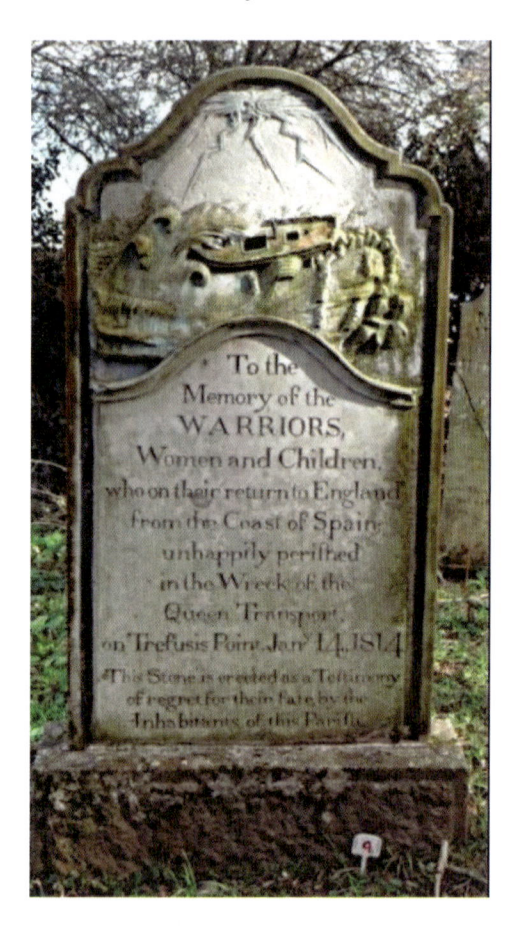

The testimonial stone in Mylor Churchyard

Trefusis point is the location of many wrecks. Over the years it has seen at least a dozen wrecks that are known of, the latest was in 2015.

In the mouth of the Helford River lies the remains of the 3,545 ton Rock Island Bridge. After a collision with the s.s. Kenosha ten miles east of the Lizard, she started taking on water. It was being towed to Falmouth but thinking it might sink in Falmouth Port, they headed for the Helford River. It sank within the river mouth, in around 8m of water, low tide. There were numerous attempts to right the ship which all failed. It was eventually reduced to scrap with explosives.

1891 saw some of the worst weather the UK had ever seen. The most extreme weather was during May, where, in one week the temperatures varied between 18C and -25C. During that winter many ships met their end around the U.K. One of those was the four masted sailing ship, the s.v. Bay of Panama. Described as the finest ship of it's day, she crashed against the rocks near Nare Point on March 10th. The following morning the Bay of Panama was a sorrowful sight, twenty eight people perished including the captain and his wife.

Bay of Panama on the rocks

Another four masted sailing ship that came to grief near Falmouth was the Andromeda. She was heading for Falmouth during a southerly gale, the ship's message for a pilot to take her into Falmouth wasn't received. It was 1915, during the Great War, the captain didn't want to enter the port unguided. No pilot came, the winds increased and drove her farther down the coast, she came ashore on Porthmellin Head. The 1,762 ton ship became a complete wreck.

Andromeda on Porthmellin Head

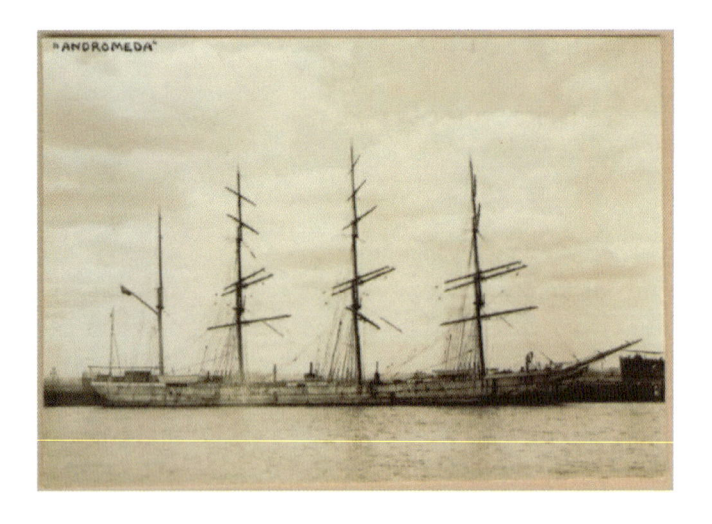

Andromeda before the wrecking

The Hera was another four masted sailing barque, in stormy conditions they looked for the light of St Anthony or the Lizard. Land was sighted all too late, it hit the Whelps reef just before midnight on January 31st, then sank just after midnight on February 1st, 1914. Nineteen sailors lost their lives, with five being rescued from the mast after clinging to it most of the night.

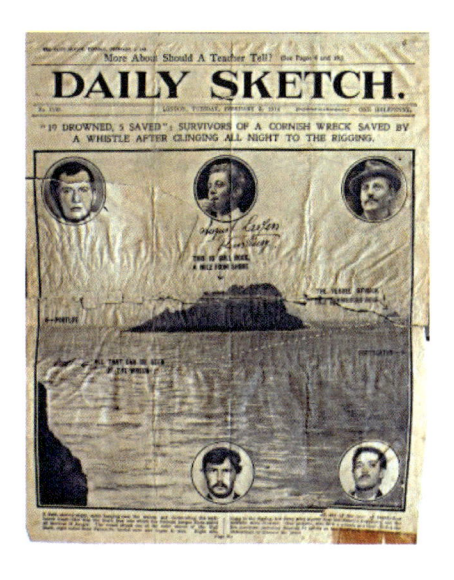

Front page of the Daily Sketch newspaper

Grave of the Hera's crew at Veryan church

November 1940 saw the diesel engined tanker, the Leon Martin, hit a mine and sink close to St Anthony's head. The 1,951 ton ship is now spread around so much, it is barely noticeable by any sonar equipment.

Another mine victim, this time during WWI, was the Dutch steamship, the s.s. Epsilon. The 3,211 ton ship struck a mine, laid by the German U-Boat the UC-17. The wreck was right in the main shipping channel and was flattened to clear it. It was then blown apart even more, the bomb squad disposed of a mine within the remains of the wreck area. The ships boilers and a several bits of the superstructure, including some large parts of the stern, are about all that remain.

ss Epsilon after coming into contact with a mine

After a collision with the s.s. Siri in March 1918, the N.G. Petersen sank close to Falmouth harbour. The N.G. Petersen was at anchor at the time. It's 1,900 ton cargo of iron ore remains but little of the 1,282 ton ship is visible.

In 1939 the 4,155 ton s.s. Stanwood came into Falmouth Docks for repairs. While there, the cargo of coal caught fire. It was towed to the north bank, a shallow area close to Mylor, where they opened the sea cocks to flood the ship and put the fire out. They intended to re-float her but she keeled over and partially slid down the bank. It was heavily salvaged and then dynamited after the war, as what remained, was deemed a hazard to shipping.

The Mitera Marigo is the biggest ship to come to grief around Falmouth. She was a 9,200 ton Greek freighter that had a collision at sea with the German ship, the Fritz Thyssen, in 1959. The captain refused any help to salvage the ship and it eventually made it into the Carrick Roads unaided. Still taking on water, the captain eventually gave permission for help but the tugs water pumps couldn't handle the volume of water either. It sank while moored to the Crossroads buoy. In 1962, commercial salvors removed most of the wreck and cargo.

In December 1917, the 4,610 ton s.s. Volnay, was torpedoed by the German submarine UC-64. Carrying wartime rations and munitions to Plymouth, she moored up near Porthallow Bay, taking on water faster than thought she foundered half a mile from the shore. Two separate attempts were made to reduce her as a hazard to shipping. It was more likely it was to destroy the anti-personnel shells on board, many of which remain.

s.s. Volnay at sea

The last wreck we will mention here, is the Caroni Rivers. This 7,807 ton, 139m long oil tanker came into Falmouth harbour for repairs. On her first sea trial she struck a mine, dropped the night before. Attempts were made to tow her in but she was taking on water too fast. She was then broken up by explosives to clear the shipping channel. The Caroni Rivers now lies in two major sections underwater, one part seems to be mixed with the remains of a small steamship, maybe an old steam fishing trawler.

It is estimated that there are over one hundred and forty wrecks in Falmouth Bay and the Carrick Roads. Not including Gerrans Bay or the Manacles. Most are only known due to a line or two in a local newspaper of the time. The wrecks we have mentioned, all have more known history than that, with known wreck locations. There are people actively looking for any evidence regarding these un-found wrecks, including the author, it's not always easy.

Falmouth Bay's Marine Life

A Unique Area

The wildlife around Falmouth is extremely varied

Falmouth Bay's unique position of having two different river estuaries feeding into the bay from the north and the west sides, brings a lot of nutrients into the area, to feed a wide variety of life. Apart from the microscopic plankton, which is everywhere, there are certain life forms which are at home in Falmouth Bay in huge numbers.

Falmouth Reef Scene with Pink Sea Fans.

Maerl, a coralline red algae, is in abundance around the bay and estuaries. A large Maerl bed exist in the Fal estuary, near St Mawes. Another Maerl bed covers a large area just south of Pendennis Point. The Percuil River and the Helford River also have healthy Maerl beds. Maerl can also be found dotted around the bay but not in any great depth, as it is within the other beds. Maerl creates a unique habitat for many small creatures, it can act as a nursery for many species as well. The beds come alive at night, with hundreds of eyes being reflected by torch light.

Pink Maerl bed.

There are actually two species of Maerl in the area. The difference is hardly noticeable, one has thicker nodules than the other. Maerl is exceedingly slow growing, at around just 1mm per year. Parts of some Maerl beds have been carbon dated at nearly 5,500 years old.

Parts of Falmouth Bay's sea bed are completely covered in Brittle Stars. These small creatures are related to starfish, they carpet the sea bed in their millions. The central disc of the Brittle star comes in a wide variety of colours, they could be blue or orange and white. Their legs can be seen pointing upwards trying to collect suspended organisms, that may have washed down and out of the rivers. Feather stars can be found on the more exposed rocky areas like the Manacles. Other starfish include the common starfish, Bloody Henry, Spiny Starfish and the Seven Armed Starfish. Spiny starfish can grow quite large, some measure nearly 60cm across, Brittle stars are quite small with the centre discs measuring around 20-25mm.

Brittle Stars

Bloody Henry with Dead Mans Fingers

Common Starfish

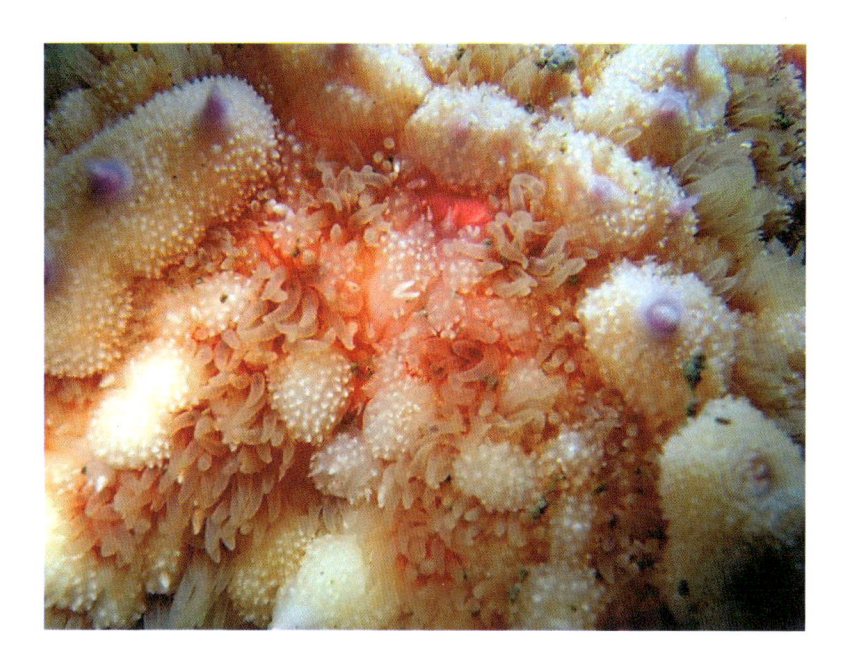

Close up of a Spiny Starfish

Brittle Star with a colourful centre disc

Urchins are closely related to starfish and the common Edible Sea Urchin can be found on the deeper rocks and reefs. Although they feed mainly on seaweed they seem to stay well away from the low water mark.

Edible Sea Urchin

Sea Cucumbers are also common, including the surface crawling cotton spinner, which likes similar locations to the Sea Urchin, the reefs below the kelp but not too deep. The mud and rock dwelling, burrowing sea cucumber also seems to like similar deeper rocky locations.

Cotton Spinner Sea Cucumber

Burrowing sea cucumber

Around the rocky coastline there are many types of red, green and brown seaweed (algae) including Kelp, Wracks, Sugar Kelp and Thongweed.

Kelp forest on the left, a common sight around Falmouth

There are also Sea Grass beds within the Helford River, Swanpool Beach, Gyllyngvase Beach and in the Percuil River near Carricknath point. The Sea Grass beds are home to many small species, that make their home in the sea grass. The beds get visited by creatures like Cuttlefish and Nudibranchs. Sea Grass beds are an extremely important habitat, a good place for juvenile fish to hide from prey.

Sea Grass beds, a extremely important habitat

Along the rocks fish such as Wrasse, Pollock and Whiting patrol the water, while Blennies & Long-Spined Sea Scorpions wait on the rocks and in the cracks. Conger Eels are usually at home amongst the wrecks or deeper rock crevasses, usually accompanied with a group of prawns. Bib and Larger Pollack are common fish found shoaling around the wrecks. Rock Cooks and the Goldsinny are common around the deeper reefs but can be found almost anywhere. Tiny Two-spotted Clingfish attach themselves to rocks and shells, while the Greater Pipefish lays on the sea bed in shallow water relatively motionless. Dragonets are also found on the sand as well as many types of Gobies.

Pollack

Wrasse

Squid

Pipefish

Tompot Blennie

Sea Hare

Long Spined Scorpion Fish

Of the fish in Falmouth Bay, the male Cuckoo Wrasse is by far the most colourful with it's electric blue and orange colouring. The Corkwing and Ballen Wrasse are also very common with interesting colours and markings.

Male Cuckoo Wrasse

There are many types of crabs around the bay, across the sea bed you can find Hermit Crabs, Leach's Spider Crabs and Brown Crabs. Green Swimming Crabs and Harbour Crabs tend to be closer to the rocks or within the estuaries. Spider Crabs can be found either within the kelp or moving almost en-mass across the sea bed as they move to and from their mating grounds.

Hermit Crabs with symbiotic cloak anemones.

Spider Crab

Brown Crab

Leach's spider crab

Lobsters usually, but not always, restrict themselves to the safe haven of a wreck or a deep crack/crevasse, whereas Squat Lobsters can be found within the rocks or on rocks along the river beds.

Lobster

Squat Lobster

A range of Nudibranchs (sea slugs) are usually found on the deeper rocks but Sea Hares can be found in abundance on sea bed in the Helford River. Nudibranchs come in a wide variety of colours and shapes. Sea Lemons can be found both on the sand and on the rocks, all around the bay.

Below are some of Falmouth's local Nudibranchs

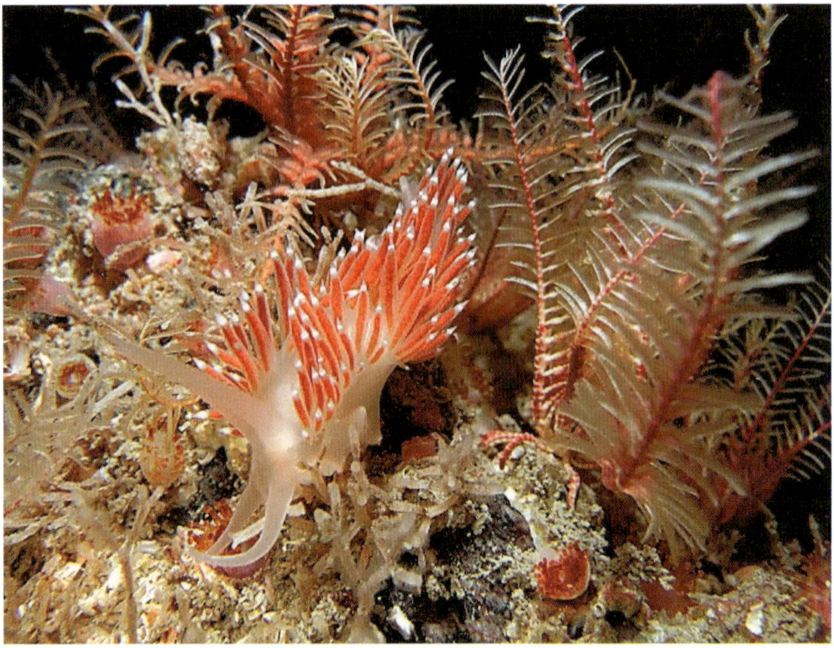

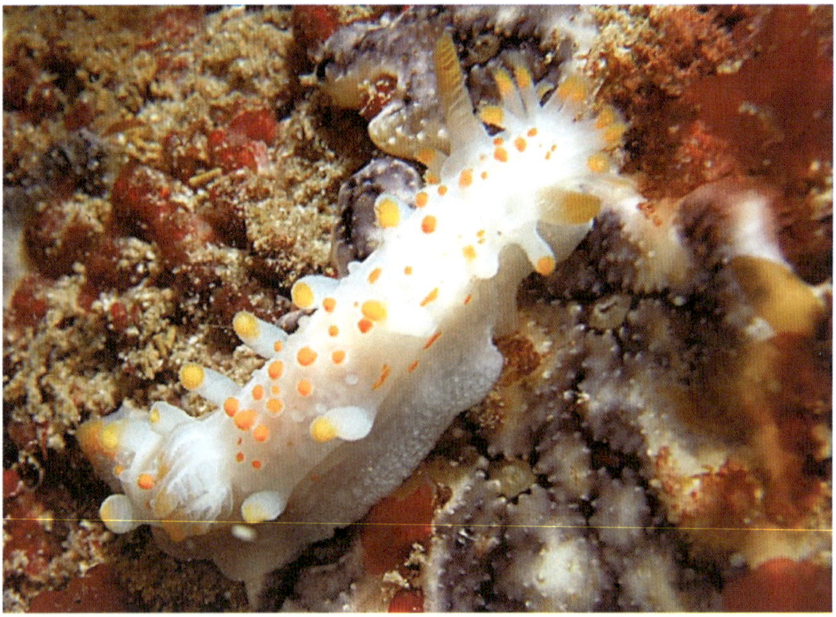

Seasonal visitors such as Bass are rarely spotted but are regularly caught by fishermen. Mackerel comes and go throughout the year and sometimes you can see the sea boiling as they feed close to the surface. Schools of Sardines leave a tell tale sign of an oil slick on the surface of the water.

Mackerel feeding

Plaice

The biggest seasonal visitor is the Basking Shark. This massive fish wanders into the area around late April looking for the Plankton Bloom. During the summer of 2006 there were so many Basking Sharks around the bay, that they became a danger to small boats. Basking Sharks are a protected species by law, any boat owners would have been in serious trouble, legally and maybe physically, if their boat came into contact with one at speed. Blue sharks are around during the summer months but usually stay well offshore. Sun Fish of all sizes also visit the area during the summer months.

Basking Shark

Other members of the shark family, such as the Lesser Spotted Dogfish (Cat Shark) and the Thornback Ray are much more common. Spotted Rays do appear but are less common than the Thornback Ray. Thornback Rays come into the estuaries in large quantities during the spring, to feed and breed.

Thornback Ray

The larger Bull Huss can also be found around the bay. Juvenile Thornback Rays and juvenile Bull Huss can sometimes be found in the Fal Estuary.

Bull Huss

Angler Fish (Monkfish) rarely come into the bay but in 2011 there were a lot of smaller ones around, lying in camouflage on the coarse sand. Large Monkfish can be found in deeper waters but do get seen in shallower waters.

Large Monkfish

Red Gurnard (below) also like waiting on the coarse sand, using their lower three rays of the pectoral fins, they 'walk' away as divers get close.

Flatfish such as Plaice, Flounder, Dover Sole, Topknots, Dab, Brill and Turbot can be found scattered around the Bay and Helford River.

Topknot

Cod are occasionally sighted just lying on the coarse sand. Ling can be found around the wrecks, juvenile Ling can be spotted within the Fal estuary.

Compass Rose Jellyfish, Comb Jellyfish and Blue Jellyfish are seasonal, with the Blue and Comb Jellies being quite prolific at times. The very large Barrel Jellyfish and the long Lions Mane Jellyfish are infrequent visitors. During the summer of 2014 the Barrel Jellyfish were quite prolific.

Comb Jelly

Blue Jellyfish

Barrel Jellyfish with shoaling fish

Barrel Jellyfish

Compass Rose jellyfish next to a diver

Cuttlefish can be found at most times of the day while Octopus tend to be nocturnal. Other nocturnal life includes Red Mullet, which appear in quantity after sunset. Even fresh water Eels have been spotted after sundown.

Cuttlefish

Red Mullet

Molluscs are found everywhere. King and Queenie Scallops can be seen on the coarse sand as can Whelks.

Queenie Scallop

King Scallop on Maerl

Almost every mooring rope has a covering of mussels, everything in the shallows ends up with a coating of Barnacles, including boat hulls. Limpets also spend their time on the shallow rocks. Whilst you can only see the tell tale signs of Cockles and Clams, which are buried in the sand. Razor Clams are also buried in the sand, usually just deeper than low water but some get caught out on low spring tides.

Gobie in Mussel shell

Squid are occasionally spotted but are more nocturnal, their eggs show a recent visit.

Squid eggs

The Candy Striped Flatworm isn't common but can be spotted on the deeper wrecks and reefs. The furry Sea Mouse can be spotted on the sea bed at various places around the Bay.

Candy Stripe Flatworm

Anemones are almost everywhere. Jewel Anemones come in an amazing range of colours and can completely cover the deeper rocks and reefs.

Jewel anemones covering the rocks

Jewel Anemones

Plumose Anemones can do the same to wrecks.

White Plumrose Anemone

Plumose anemones on the Hera wreck

Dead Man's Fingers and Red Fingers are species of soft corals, they can be found in abundance over wrecks and reefs.

Dead Man's Fingers

Red Fingers

Pink Sea Fans are also at home on both wrecks and reefs but tend to be seen only on the deeper wrecks and the deeper reefs. These rare hard corals are not so rare around Falmouth.

Pink Sea Fan

Pink sea fans on the wreck of the Mohegan

Tube Worms and burrowing sea Anemones prefer the faster moving waters of the estuaries but can also be found in different parts of the sandy sea bed.

Tube Worm

Beadlet and Dahlia Anemones can be found across the rocks at most depths. Strawberry and Snakelock Anemones prefer the shallower waters.

Dahlia Anemone

Devonshire Cup Corals (below) are common and can be extremely colourful especially when photographed with the camera's strobe light.

There is an abundance of life, including an extremely rare worm Anemone Scolanthis Callimorphus, photographed in the Fal estuary, pictured below.

Scolanthis Callimorphus

Last but not least, our biggest local marine animals, Seals and Dolphins. A small group of Atlantic Grey Seals live around the area, they can usually be seen at low water around Black Rock, basking in the sun. At high water they are hunting food, their heads can be seen popping up along the coastline and even in Mylor Harbour.

Grey Seal

Bottlenose Dolphins were common visitors and often escorted boats around the bay, nowadays it is Common Dolphins that are coming in closer, riding the bow wave of a boat.

Common Dolphin escorting our boat

Farther offshore Pilot Whales and Minke Whales can be spotted. Harbour Porpoises are also quite common around the area.

There are many species that haven't had a mention, there are also several genus that haven't either. The Genus of Sponges, Sea Squirts, Hydroids and Bryozoans are plentiful around the bay but have not been included within this guide. There are so many different forms of life around Falmouth, it would need a book of it's own to try to cover them. There are books about the life around Cornwall, which are well worth reading and are mentioned in the 'further reading' section at the end of this book. Most of the species mentioned in this guide are mainly ones with 'common names', therefore, they are only a sample of their genus found in Falmouth Bay.

Sponge

Bryozoan

Octopus

Nudibranch Eggs

Sandalled Anemone

Ross Coral (Bryozoan)

Snakelock Anemone, there is a Leach's crab hiding behind it

Strawberry Anemone

Colonial Sea Squirt

Falmouth Bay's Snorkelling and Shore Diving

So Much Choice

A Good Selection of Wrecks and Reefs

Falmouth Bay is protected from the predominant south westerly winds by the Lizard Peninsula. This makes it likely that you will get favourable conditions to go snorkelling or shore diving. The worst times to try and go off the beaches around Falmouth, is during an easterly or southerly wind. These winds will bring waves, in the past, they have also brought many wrecks.

There are at least three German WWI Submarine (U-Boats) remains, a 5,077 ton WWI oil tanker and a 422 ton fishing trawler at shallow depths, that can be snorkelled or dived from the shore. There are many other wrecks but most have very little left that is recognisable.

The sea bed shelves slowly around the area, you will have to swim a long way out to get much deeper than 10m. Visibility varies from 1m to up to 10m. Marine life is exceedingly varied as detailed in the Marine Life section. Even at these relatively shallow depths, there are a wide of things to see from Nudibranchs to Seals, if you're lucky that is.

This chapter will start at the most northerly site and work south. In reality, you can snorkel almost anywhere, shore diving requires good access to the water and close parking. The whole of the shore line is all worth snorkelling, this guide is designed to make sure you don't miss something special or unique.

Going snorkelling

Surface marker buoys are always recommended. The snorkellers above are a mixture of freedivers and snorkellers. Using a high visibility buoy allows all surface traffic to see you more easily. There can be a lot of traffic around the bay, including stand up paddle boarders, kayakers, wind surfers and any amount of boat users of all types. Most boats will stay clear of the shore line, kayakers and paddle boarders may explore the shore quite closely. Along the main sea front from Castle Beach to Swanpool Beach, there are a series of buoys. These buoys are speed markers for boats, restricting their speed to 4 knots, it doesn't stop them coming close to shore.

Going for a shore dive at the Silver Steps

Falmouth's most popular shore dive is the "Silver Steps", it is also an excellent place to snorkel. The Silver Steps relate to the bright granite steps going down to the sea off Pendennis Headland, pictured above. To get there, head along Castle Drive, the one way system around Pendennis headland. The first landmark on the left is a long lay-by, with a view over the dockyard. Then, a little farther around at the point there is a car park, with views over Falmouth Bay, go passed this too. A few hundred metres farther along, just before the road becomes two way, there is a lay-by on the left (pictured on the next page). Park in that lay-by, as close as you can to the start, it is free too.

Lay-by on the left, park there.

The path to the steps is just to the left of the lay-by looking out to sea. The path splits into two before it reaches the steps. It is possible to enter the water from the left hand or right hand path and steps. Divers will enter the water more safely from the well trodden right hand path and steps. There are more than a dozen steps down, for most of the way there is a heavy duty handrail to hold on to. The handrail is especially useful on the way back up.

As a snorkeller, the left hand path will take you closer to one of the submarine wrecks, the UB-86. UB-86 is one of several submarines remains left around Falmouth's shore. At low water, part of the submarine even breaks the surface. The submarines have all been heavily salvaged over the years, but, there is enough left to make it worthwhile spending some time exploring them.

Part of UB-86 on a low spring tide

Fish do like to hide within the shelter and protection of any wrecks too. In the gully to the right of UB-86, looking from shore, are the remains of another submarine, the UB-112. The most noticeable part of the submarine remaining is a large three pronged fork, possibly part of the hydro-vane hinge. The top of the UB-112 is around 2m at low water. There is much more left of the UB-86 than there is of the UB-112 though.

East of UB-86 is an interesting gully with a tiny cave at the end, within the cave are the remains of a small motorbike. The bike does get buried in sand now and then. At around a maximum depth of 3m the cave almost empties on low spring tides. Farther east of the U-Boats, there is a large rock pool, known locally as the 'hole in the wall'. It is situated a few hundreds metres before the lay-by mentioned above, where there is a gap in the fence to a path. This leads down to the rocks, you can then walk back towards the hole in the wall. You can enter the rock pool, it is deep enough for a stride entry, then swim through a shallow underwater arch that takes you out to the sea.

As a diver, it is safest to enter the water down the granite steps and across the well worn rocks. Swim along the bottom of the gully, until you reach the sand. From here you have some options. If you turn right, you can swim along the rocky kelp covered reef. There are many small rocky outcrops which make it an interesting dive. Another option is to head straight out, passed the coarse sand and onto a stony area. Within this area you can find the odd scallop. On the coarse sand there is a boiler from a steam fishing trawler, it sank around 1849 and can easily be missed. Swimming to the left about a hundred metres, is the gully where the remains of UB-112 are.

Part of UB-112

Head back out onto the sand, keeping the reef on your left, until you get to the next gully. There you will find the remains of the UB-86 as mentioned above. It stretches quite a way up the gully.

Heading back out onto the sand once again and into the next gully, which is where the cave can be found. The cave is very shallow and does not go in very far, it is scenic, easy enough for a scuba diver, for the more experienced snorkeller. When the sand shifts, you can see the remains of the small motorbike in the entrance.

One of the caves on Pendennis

The Silver Steps is not really recommended at low water for divers, mainly because the entry point is uneven and rocky when exposed. It is dived at low water, just mind where you tread, the sea weeds are slippery.

The next location for a snorkel or a shore dive is off of Castle Beach. Castle Beach is in front of the Falmouth Hotel, just a little farther along the coast from the 'Silver Steps'. It is the location of another German WWI submarine, the UC-92. The submarine is not far offshore, it's around 100m to the far end of the wreck from the lower wall. At high water you can swim over the reef straight to the wreck. At lower states of the tide, it is best to head about 20m south of the lower slope. There is a sandy bottomed gap in the reef which makes for easy entry, the sand can move and sometimes it gets filled with detached sea weed. You can find the

U-Boat by swimming along the reef to the north, it is usually covered in kelp and can be hard to spot. The wreck lies at ninety degrees to the shore, bow to the shore. Before the winter storms of 2013/14 you could line up the left hand edge of the Falmouth Hotel, with the left hand side of the cafe and swim out. Those winter storms demolished that cafe. The replacement cafe is slightly to the right of the previous one, so the new transit is to line the left hand side of the cafe up with the left hand side of the furthest left windows, as per the image below.

At low water spring tides, the shallowest part of the wreck breaks the surface, the deepest is around 6m at high water. Wessex Archaeology completed a project on this U-Boat during the summer of 2013, identifying it as the remains of UC-92, the only mine-laying submarine to be wrecked in the area. The six, one metre diameter mine shafts are clearly visible, at the bow end of the submarine, closest to shore.

Castle Beach is dive-able at any state of tide, there are no noticeable currents.

Parking is usually available along the roadside, above the cafe. The cafe and the Public toilet are open all summer with restricted hours during the winter.

Along the coast another half a mile is Gyllyngvase beach, our next location. Gyllyngvase has some pleasant reefs at each end of the beach. The north end reef runs all the way to Castle Beach, passed Tunnel Beach. Periodically Seals can be seen patrolling this area. The reef to the southern end is interesting enough, but, a little farther around the reef, there is the remains of a wreck, the 5,077 ton oil tanker, the s.s. Ponus. The remains of the wreck are well broken and spread over a large area. The biggest piece of wreck stands around two to three metres off the sea bed.

Part of the remains of the s.s. Ponus

The previous way of finding the wreck was by lining up a sign on the beach with a tree, the sign was another victim of the 2013/14 winter storms. The council then removed the the buoy, placing it on the wall. Now the transit is a little harder to see. The following image lines a tree up in the car park, with the left purple gate post.

Line the left purple gate post with the tree shown.

The only other line of sight (transit), are the steps to the right of the restaurant at Swanpool, becoming visible around the point.

Once you find the wreck you can swim around the area for a long time, finding more and more of it as you go. It does have a good covering of kelp, so it can be hard to spot the remains down there. It is spread over an area of at least 50m by 40m with steel plates, pipes and ribs half buried in sand. The sand can shift and parts of the wreck get covered and uncovered. The top of wreck can break the surface on a low spring tide, maximum depth is 8m at high water. The best place to park for the southern reef, is on the road just behind the Queen Mary Gardens. You can then walk around the southern end of the gardens to the beach.

Queen Mary Gardens, park on the road to the left of the picture

There is a wall by the beach, just as you get onto the sand, it is an ideal place for a diver to put their dive kit on before entering the water.

For access to the northern end, you can park along the main road and go down the steps. A snorkeller can also enter the water at Tunnel Beach, entering the reef mid way between Castle Beach and Gyllyngvase Beach.

Gyllyngvase Beach is dive-able at any state of tide, there are no noticeable currents.

Next along is Swanpool Beach, Swanpool is a very easy, lazy dive and a very easy place to snorkel. Especially at high tide. From the car park to the water can be as little as a 25m walk. The southern reef is plain and simple, usually with large shoals of small fish during early summer, as well as the normal reef fish of wrasse and pollack. The reef winds its way in and out all the way to the point about 400m away. There can be currents around the point, although it would be a long swim for a diver, it is best avoided. Even for strong and experienced snorkeller, the current around the point mid tide can be too much.

Swanpool Beach near low tide, a bit too shallow to dive

The north side reef is slightly shallower than the southern side, at high water there is a very shallow arch, just a metre or so deep, that you can go through. On high springs you can snorkel around the back of the island and out through the arch. You can dive through the arch but it is almost impossible to go around the arch in dive gear. At low water you can walk through the arch.

In the section between the two reefs there are some sea grass beds, which can attract all sorts of little critters and even the occasional ray.

Sea Grass Beds at Swanpool Beach

Maenporth Beach also has a wreck, the Ben Asdale, a 422 ton fishing trawler that was wrecked in 1978. It is very shallow and about a three hundred metre swim out. It is a long distance to cover for a shore dive but it is an excellent snorkel, the reef to it can be interesting too. The wreck lies behind rocks along the left hand side, the north side of the cove, it is not visible from the beach. At low water you can climb across the rocks to get to the wreck, then walk around most of the remains of the Ben Asdale. Just passed the wreck is a tiny cave, you can snorkel a little way in, or dive in a little farther. Seals have been seen inside the cave by divers, in the cave mouth is another piece of wreckage, probably from the Ben Asdale as well.

You can also walk along the cliff path to see the remains of the wreck from above. You have to make your way through some bushes, to get to the ledge above it though. The south side of Maenporth is also quite interesting, there are several gullies and caves to explore, even a small swim through. The car park on the beach makes easy access to the water.

Remains of the Ben Asdale at low water

Ben Asdale winch viewed at high tide

Bream Cove is along the coast path about a mile from Maenporth. Although there is a wreck in the area, there is little left, except for bits of the cement cargo on the rocks. To the left are some nice gullies, to the right is a swim out along the reef towards Rosemullion Head. It is a good place for a snorkel but a bit of a hike to take any diving equipment.

The last not to be missed location is the Helford River. The beaches of Grebe and Durgan are just a couple of hundred metres apart, on the north side of the Helford River. Durgan has a lot of moorings to swim around while Grebe has no moorings at all. They both have Sea Grass beds with a wide variety of life. The Helford River is a voluntary special area of conservation, mainly because of the sea grass and the variety of life it shelters. It is best to dive or snorkel just before slack water, slack water is around one hour after high or low water. Head into the opposite direction of the next tide, go east if before high water, go west if before low water, so you can swim back with the tide when it turns. If you don't, you may struggle to get back to where you started. The maximum depth is around 6m off of either beach. Parking isn't easy as the car park is at the top of the hill, don't park anywhere else, as the police do patrol the area. You can drop your dive gear off by the beach, before parking in the car park and walking back. The trip is worth it if you like marine life. Thornback Rays and Cuttlefish have been spotted while just snorkelling on the surface.

Durgan Beach at high water

There are other places to shore dive around Falmouth but most are a long way to walk with your equipment, or the currents are too much if you miss slack water. There are also many other very interesting sites to snorkel. You can wander along the cliff paths and find little coves that no-one visits. This section of the guide only covers the easy access and the 'not to be missed sites'.

All the above are obviously suitable for freedivers too. An area that is good for both snorkellers and freedivers, is around St Anthony's lighthouse. There are rocks and gullies to explore around the rocky island in front of the lighthouse, there are more nice gullies northwards of the lighthouse, within the Carrick Roads.

Falmouth's Reef Dives

Colourful and Lively

Reef and Non-Wreck Dives

Falmouth has a lot of non wreck dives worth doing, even without the Manacles reef system. The Manacles' has its own section, as it is a big area with many sites to dive. In this section we will be looking at dive sites around Falmouth, that are not wreck based. From shallow caves to sites where you can find cannon balls fired from a local castle, Falmouth has a lot to offer. We will include Gerrans Bay as well as Falmouth Bay, as it is so close to Falmouth itself.

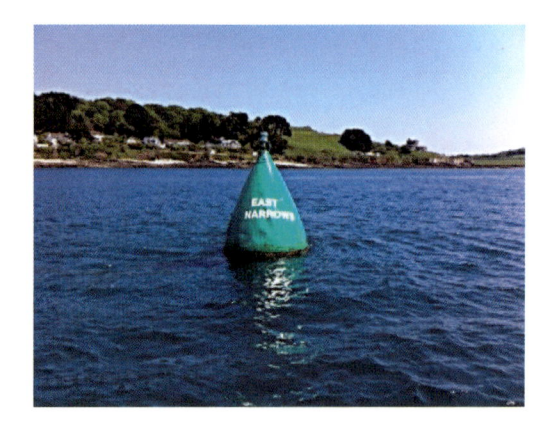

The East Narrows is a popular dive site, mainly because it is so close to the harbours and moorings around Falmouth, it is also dive-able in a moderate easterly wind. The dive normally starts on top of the east side bank, between 6-15m. Most divers will then descend down the slope to the bottom of the channel, or to a pre-planned depth. A maximum depth of 38m can be achieved at high water, on a spring tide. For a hundred metres or so south of the East Narrows buoy, there are a series of vertical walls from 15m down to 33m. There is a lot of life tucked into the nooks and crannies. Sandy slopes can take you down, along the wall and back up again. The dive is best finished in the shallows to the east, on the Maerl beds, not only is it best but is actually required by the local harbour authority. The Maerl beds are full of small critters, like squat lobsters and prawns. At night, a hundred eyes reflect your torchlight back at you from within the Maerl.

St Anthony's lighthouse is at the eastern entrance of the Fal Estuary, just in front of it is a rock, called Shag Rock. Locals refer to it a 'Fraggle Rock', due to the fact that the lighthouse was used in the opening sequence of the program of the same name.

St Anthony's Lighthouse with Shag Rock

The diving around the rock is fairly shallow with some interesting overhangs and a couple of interesting gullies. There are two swim through caves there. The longest tunnel cave goes through Shag Rock. The entrance is 2m below the 'V' formed by Shag Rock and the little rock to the south of it. The entrance looks more like a rock pool. Once you put your head inside, look to the right and a feint glow will appear. The tunnel cave is about 25m long, at about the half way point, there is an exit in the cave ceiling. From the entrance the cave opens up wider and wider, with light coming through cracks in the roof. Half way along the gully behind Shag Rock, at the far side, there is a tiny swim through arch. Maximum depth is around 8m, tides are unpredictable, eddy currents can run the opposite way of the actual tide.

Inside Fraggle Cave

Out of the Fal Estuary and to the left, eastwards, the next site of interest is the Seal Caves. A couple of shallow caves, where a few seals are known to hang out at high tide, we see them there, more often than not. Maximum depth again, is around 8m.

A little farther east and we have "Shore's Rock", a small rock island with some very nice gullies, named after a sailor who died there in 1851.

Shore's Rock area

A perfect place for a chilled out relaxing dive, or ambient light photography. Maximum depth again, is about 8m.

Next location covered is a little farther east along the coast. Killigerran Head, another shallow reef with some interesting topography. A gully close to the land has been known to have some stunning visibility. Another 8m deep dive, if you wander off away from the shore you may get 10m.

A few miles farther east and we reach Gull Rock and the Whelps Reef, at the eastern edge of Gerrans Bay. Gull Rock has two caves next to each other, ones goes into the island around 20m, the other around 5m. Quite often there are seals in the entrance. Next to Gull Rock is a smaller rock island, on it's landward side there is a 10m deep wall, covered in Jewel Anemones. Both sites can easily be covered in one dive.

The Whelps are a row of rock pinnacles, gradually disappearing off deeper as you go south of Gull Rock.

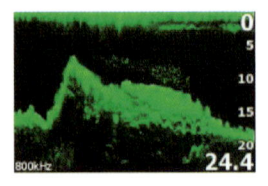

Sonar view of part of the Whelps reef

Covered in jewel anemones and dead mans fingers, the Whelps are a very scenic dive with a maximum depth of around 30m. On the western side of the Whelps there is a small 12m pinnacle, rising up from the 25m deep sea bed. The western side has a marvellous array of marine life and corals. Slightly to the east of the Whelps is a sloping reef, starting at 25m, rising up to around 18m. Nicknamed Holland Rock, by a now retired boat skipper, due to the fact a group from Holland used to like diving there. There is a gully that is easy to follow up the slope, it has been described as being better than any other reef around.

On the way back from the eastern edge of Gerrans Bay, we come across the Bizzies reef. The inner Bizzies are a pair of very shallow kelp covered pinnacles, just a few metres deep, the outer Bizzies is at the southern edge of the reef at around 36m depth. Covered in Dead Mans Fingers as well as Red Fingers, combined the inner and outer Bizzies are an impressive huge sprawling reef. The outer pinnacles have vertical walls that are covered in jewel anemones. Between the outer pinnacles lies a 27m deep sand bottomed gully, with a vertical wall on one side and a steeply sloping side opposite. The gully heads south from the flat sandy seabed to deeper part of the reef, which is a series of shallower sandy bottomed gullies which head further to the east as well. Going north through the outer pinnacles, the reef slowly shallows, over rocks covered in life.

Outer Bizzies Gully

Where Gerrans Bay meets Falmouth Bay, at the west end of the Bizzies reef, is the Old Wall. The Old Wall is a slowly shelving pinnacle, best described as more like a small underwater hill. Around the Old Wall, the depth is between 30-36m on most sides except the north side where it reaches about 17m. The top of the old wall is around 12m at high water. The deeper part has a similar covering of life as the Bizzies, the shallower areas are covered in kelp. It has been used as a dumping ground in the past, it is surprising what 'rubbish' you can find there. Anything from a brass valve to a fifty litre gas cylinder.

Falmouth Bay's seabed is mainly flat and sandy, there are a few rocky outcrops. The rocky parts that are there, are not too exciting and do not stand up very high, except for the Wrigglers. The Wrigglers are two pinnacles, one stands up nearly vertical from the 44m seabed to 26m, the other peaks at 32m. Although a lot of divers prefer to dive wrecks when deep diving, these deep pinnacles are worth a visit. They are both very colourful and covered in life, as good as many of the more well known sites.

Just north of the Wrigglers is a small pinnacle, called 'Twin Peaks'. It stands nearly 8m high and is the remains of a fallen stone stack, the area around the pinnacle is covered in boulders, which does create homes for fish and other critters.

Reef scene

The other areas that are of interest around the bay are the cannon ball site, Rosemullion Head and the Helford river. The cannon ball site is an area just over a mile south of Pendennis Castle. It is believed to be the approximate location of a possible floating target for the castle's guns, hundreds of twenty four pound cannon balls have been found and recovered over the years, there's still plenty left. There are also several sixty four pounder shells, fired from a breech loading gun that was installed in 1878. The area has ended up as a dumping ground over the years, all sorts of items have been found from a Dutch onion bottle dating 1680-1720 to a large diesel engine turbo.

Onion bottle, dating between 1680-1720, now a national monument

One of the interesting items found on the cannon ball site.

The area is close to what is on the nautical charts as the 'spoil ground'. In 1931, Falmouth docks were being enlarged. The contractor persuaded the authorities that the dredged material would help improve the quality of the sand on Falmouth's beaches. Whether or not it had any effect will probably never been proven one way or another, what it did do was to dump any litter from within the docks. That dumped material included a lot of bottles. Bits of glass from smashed bottles lay around the sea bed. There are also a lot of complete bottles, dozens of bottles dating before 1931 have been recovered.

Encrusted cannon ball

The area is quite unique for marine life, millions of brittle starfish cover the sea bed like a quilt in places, there's also plenty of other little critters and even scallops.

The Helford river has a few non wreck dive options. Most of the river is a Special Area of Conservation, mainly for the sea grass beds. The sea grass beds stretch from just west of Durgan beach, to the east of Grebe beach, on the north side of the river. Most of the sea grass is in less than 5m of water. The rest of the river bed is a mixture of coarse sand, shells and stones, almost in bands lying east to west along the river. It is home to a wide range of life that you don't get on the local reefs, other common visitors are Thornback rays, Sea Hares, Whelks and dogfish (cat sharks).

Scallops are found around the river bed, but, the river is a private fishery, technically any scallops removed are classed as theft. Another option is the Helford pool, an 18m deep pit that seems to have collected bottles and other bits of litter over the years. If dived just after high water it makes a pleasant drift dive, heading east, finishing up in the shallows of the river, at around 5-6m.

The last site in this section is Pencra reef. Not the most exciting of places but pleasant enough with plenty of life. In the shallows is an area known as Tol Peg, a shallow rock formation that almost looks like an old quay side. Three straight square sides, covered in jewel anemones, it's pleasant enough, especially if you like the squidgy stuff.

Crawfish (Rock Lobster) are making a comeback, after years of over fishing.

Falmouth's Wreck Dives

Shipping Disasters

Falmouth has it's fair share of wrecks.

Over the years, many ships have come to grief around Falmouth. Some were involved in a collision at sea, while others were victims of the weather. Enemy action during both wars also caused their share of shipping casualties. With a range of wrecks from 6m to 70m, Falmouth has something for everyone. This section will look at boat dives on wrecks down to 30m, with a short mention of some of the deeper wrecks. Shore dives, reef dives and the Manacles are covered in other chapters within this book. There is also a chapter just on wrecks in this book, this section is about diving the wrecks with the most remains.

The Caroni Rivers was a 7,807 ton oil tanker. It came into Falmouth for repairs, on it's first sea trial it hit a mine laid by U-34, a German submarine, the night before. Being such a large vessel, it's bridge remained out of the water. It was in the shipping lane, for traffic coming into Falmouth from the south, it had to be removed one way or another. The easiest way to remove a ship, was to blow it up, so that's what they did. After the clearance was completed, it was well scattered. It now lies in two different main areas, several hundred metres apart. The most commonly dived part is a mixture of bent and twisted metal piled up all over the place. To be honest it is almost impossible to work out which part it is. There are some boiler parts lying around, which don't belong to the Caroni Rivers. The boiler parts possibly came from a small steam trawler, which just happened to be where the Caroni Rivers foundered. The remains of the wreck do not stand up much more than a few metres, from the 25m deep sea bed. It is home to some large Conger Eels as well as plenty of different types of Wrasse. It is a good general dive with some interesting places for a rummage around.

What is believed to be the remains of a boiler from a previous wreck

The second area of the Caroni Rivers' wreckage is much smaller. There are several decent sized pieces of bent hull lying around, which can make it a little more interesting than the larger area. It would be better if there were more of it though. It has some good opportunities for some interesting camera shots, due to the angles and shapes of the wreckage, it needs to be well lit though as it is usually quite dark down there.

Between the two areas and around them as well, there are more pieces of wreckage, scattered after the demolition explosions scattered pieces everywhere. The wreckage is quite hard to pinpoint on a sonar because of this, as well as being quite flat.

The Epsilon sank in 1917 after hitting a mine laid by UC-17. The ships boilers are the most interesting and the highest parts of the dive. They are home to several Conger Eels that pop their heads out as divers pass.

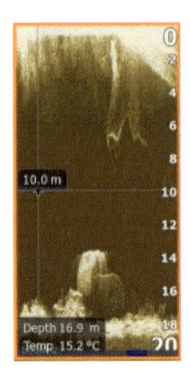

Sonar view of the Epsilon's boilers, bottom centre of the image

The wreck is quite scattered with the odd girder sticking out of the sand. Very little of the wreck's hull remains apart from a few steel plates, the stern section has the most remaining wreckage. Although the stern is fairly flat, it is still very interesting. Within the wreckage you can still see the steering quadrant, which has been separated from the rudder post. There is quite a bit of life around, including Jewel and Plumose Anemones on some of the girders and occasionally a shoal of Bib around the boilers. Maximum depth, again, is around 25m on high water.

A few miles up the coast, at the eastern edge of Gerrans Bay where it meets Veryan Bay, lies the remains of the four masted steel sailing barque, the Hera. At a maximum depth of 18m it is suitable for all divers. It also has something for everyone. The wreck is in two main sections about 20m apart, separated by the masts laying on the sea bed, almost leading the way from the bow section to the stern section. The main "attraction" has to be what the local call the "A" frame, it is the remains of the bow structure. The bow's hull plating was supposedly blown off when some salvage work was taking place. It stands nearly five meters tall and is covered in Jewel Anemones, Plumose Anemones and Dead Mans Fingers.

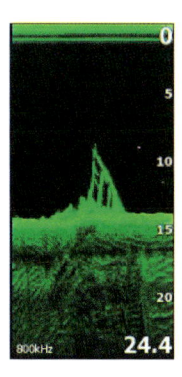

Bow of the Hera standing upright

The are usually a few Pollack cruising around the beams of the bow too. There is plenty of room to swim among the beams and get a close up view of all the life. Close to the frame is one of the ships anchors, one of the flukes is buried in the sand, the other fluke stands about 1.2m off the sea bed. There are also a couple of capstans around that area and what is thought to be the bow sprit. There is so much to see. There are two swim-throughs, one in each section of the wreck, both are quite "tight" on the exits, so be careful, check the exits are clear first.

Hera's bow, as it is now

The N.G. Petersen sank in Falmouth Bay whilst at anchor, a collision with the Norwegian s.s. Siri in 1918 was all it took. It was carrying a cargo of iron ore, most of the iron ore remains. Over the years the hull has gradually disappeared, what is left of the hull is only visible where it meets the sea bed. There are areas where there are gaps between the hull and sea bed, usually home for a Conger Eel or two. At one end there are some winches and chains visible, around the wreck there is a lot of debris. Pieces of hull, structural beams and pieces of deck machinery lie around. The wreck is easily navigable on one dive. It is at a general depth of around 24m at high tide. Towards one end of the the wreck there is a big gouge, a large ship's anchor dragged through the wreck.

A piece of the N G Petersen

The Rock Island Bridge is one of the shallowest of the usual wreck dives that are completed from a boat. After a collision with the s.s. Kenosha in 1920, it was taken under tow to Falmouth but wasn't going to make it to the port. So they towed it to the Helford, where it sank in the river mouth.

It now lies in a maximum depth of just 13m, the tallest part being around 2m off of the sea bed.

Side scan sonar image of the Rock Island Bridge

It has been heavily salvaged, the shifting sands of the Helford river cover and uncover parts of it. For a shallow dive, it has a reasonable amount of life, due to the nutrients washing down the river passed the wreck. The most popular part for divers, is that the wreckage of the Rock Island Bridge lies in healthy scallop beds. Most divers stay on the wreck some last just ten or twenty minutes, then go hunting food.

Part of the Rock Island Bridge

Lying within the Carrick Roads is the wreck of the s.s. Stanwood. A collier ship that came into Falmouth for repairs. It caught fire, then it was towed to shallow water of the north bank and deliberately sank to extinguish the fire. The fire was put out but the wreck keeled over, and slid down the bank. Then lying on the edge of the shipping channel, it was salvaged, then reduced by explosives.

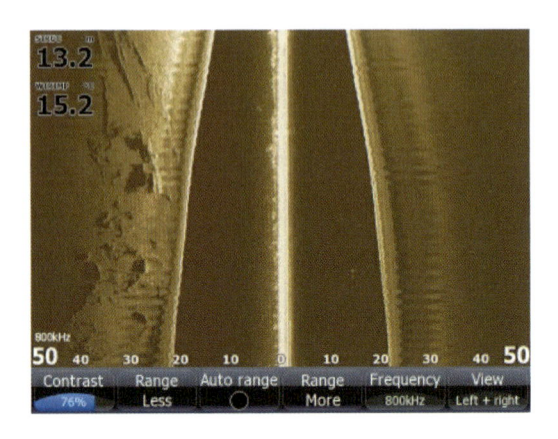

Remains of the s.s. Stanwood on the north bank slope

What is left is a large amount of twisted steel. An interesting dive that always seems to attract some big lobsters, scallops lie to the south of it in the deeper parts of the channel. Large shoals of fish hang around this wreck as well, possibly because it is the largest place of any shelter around the area. Maximum depth is around 26m, slack water is important as the current can be strong, high tide is best for a chance of some good visibility.

Last, but not least, is the s.s. Volnay. The Volnay is the most often dived wreck in the bay, as a boat dive, mainly due to it's location. It is fairly close inshore to Porthallow on the east side of the Lizard peninsula, therefore protected from some of the strong south westerly winds. It is also in an area that has little tide. The lack of tide does usually means reduced visibility though. Lying roughly NNW to SSE, it's two large boilers stand about 4m high and are it's most noticeable of the larger parts. Just behind the two boilers is a third, smaller, donkey boiler. It was a large ship at one hundred and seventeen metres long and weighing in at 4610 tons. It is spread over a large area, steel plates and spars cover the seabed.

Two attempts were made to flatten the wreck, or maybe to destroy the large quantity of anti-personnel ammunition it was carrying. The evidence of this attempted destruction is visible looking at the twisted metal.

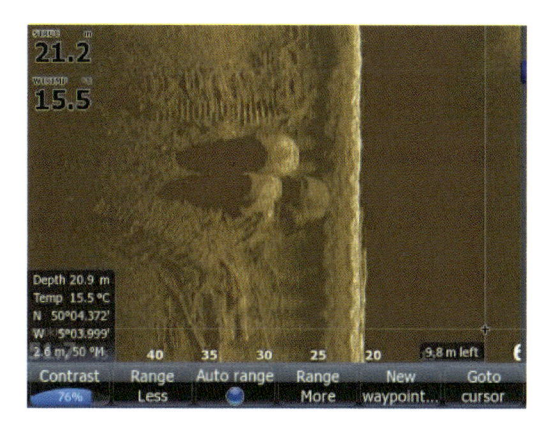

Side scan image of the boilers on the s.s. Volnay

Towards the bow you can see the remains of the chain locker with the anchor winches and chains. Similarly at the stern. At both the bow and stern the silty bottom gives way to a reef system, the higher and more interesting being at the bow. Scattered over a lot of the wreck, you can find small white balls, these are oxidised lead shot from its cargo of anti-personnel shells. The brass shell cases and brass timer heads are still being found today, you would have to dig for them now.

A diver on the s.s. Volnay

There are other shallow wrecks around the area that can be dived but rarely are. Like the s.v. Bay of Panama and the s.v. Andromeda, both were sailing ships that crashed onto the shore in bad weather, both lie in a maximum depth of 8m. Mainly covered in sea weeds, both are worth a dive but with so many good dive sites around they tend to get ignored. The Bay of Panama can be completely covered in sand, and, as the Andromeda, is quite flat. The Andromeda can be partially covered but there is always quite a few parts exposed. During the winter storms of 2013/14, 1.5m of sand was removed from the site of the Andromeda, exposing a lot more of the wreck. Several brass items were recovered, including the builders plate.

Remains of the builders plate or capstan top. It states the builders name, ship yard and the build number.

Most of the wrecks listed in the previous shore dive section have been, and still can be, dived from a boat. It saves finding a parking spot and lugging your gear across beaches. Potentially giving you more time on the sites to explore.

Within Gerrans Bay are the remains of a WWII Wellington bomber, smashed by dredgers over the years. The location is kept quiet by locals but it does get dived occasionally. There are also the so far, unfound wrecks of the Tulip 2 and the Burnside. The Burnside has proven to be one of those wrecks that just doesn't want to be found, possibly because the navy took two weeks to destroy it, after it ran aground. May be they towed it somewhere else, before sinking it.

There are virtually no wrecks between 30 and 45m within the area. There are many deeper wrecks, in the technical diving range, deeper than 45m that is. Wrecks such as 'The Lady of the Isles', sunk in 1940 after hitting a mine while under tow. Lying in around 50m, the stern section still stands but not very high, it was a small ship. HMT Rinovia is another mine victim, sank in 1940, it now lie fairly intact and upright within the 50m range, it has a large trawl net over it which has been colonised by Plumose Anemones. Close to the Rinovia is the Jersey Queen, another mine victim, as was the HMS Torrent close by. HMS Comet and the Ben Rein, also close by, were also mine victims. The Great Eastern is a large vessel lying close to the old dumping ground in around 60m, a silty area but a great dive.

Other ships in the area include the s.s. Spital, s.s. Bretonne, the Lord Snowden and the Eric Calvert. These are all good dives and there are many more, enough to keep any technical diver busy for weeks.

Manacles' Dive Sites

Hidden Dangers

Wreck Grave Yard

Over the years, the hidden pinnacles of the Manacles Reef system, have been a major hazard for all shipping. With over fifty known wrecks and countless unknown wrecks, the hidden pinnacles and small rock islands of the Manacles, is very popular with divers and fishermen. Sticking out about two miles from shore, on the eastern side of the Lizard peninsula, there can be some very strong currents, which attract a lot of marine life. With stories of haunted wrecks and rock names such as "The Voices", it conjures up an air of mystery. On a foggy day, it certainly looks an eerie and a dangerous place. At high water, there is little sign of what lies beneath. At low water, especially on a spring tide, you can see why there have been many shipping casualties in the past. Even at the lowest of spring tides there are many more rocks just a few metres under the surface.

Some of the visible rocks at low water include Shark's Fin, Carn Du, Main Voes, Gwinges and Maen Chynoweth. Hidden pinnacles include Raglans Reef, Pen-Wyn and Vase Rock. Raglans Reef, Pen-Wyn and Vase Rock all rise up from around 40m and reach within a few metres of the surface. All are covered in carpets of multi coloured Jewel Anemones, as well as Pink Sea Fans and Dead Mans Fingers. There is barely a square inch of rock showing, they are all covered in life.

Although the Manacles are covered in wrecks, there is very little left of most of them. One wreck that is both well known and well dived, is the Mohegan. A massive four masted liner, that for some reason, steered a wrong course. Instead of being ten miles south of the Manacles, it came to grief after hitting the Manacles at full speed in 1898. Initially hitting the sunken pinnacle of Pen-Wyn Rock, where she lost her rudder, she continued until she hit the Voices, Maen Voes. A massive hole was ripped in her side and she quickly sunk, taking one hundred and two souls with her. Over the years, time, tide and salvage has taken its toll. The engine was removed in the 1960's, when there were virtually no recreational divers on her. Twenty years later there were up to two hundred divers a day on her, nowadays, she can have several boats at once around in the summer.

Sprawling over a massive area, her four boilers stand four metres proud of the sea bed. Although it looks like there are only three boilers, two smaller boilers are back to back.

Close to the centre you can make out the three round shapes of the boilers

The visible wreckage is stacked up around three or four metres high, in places you can see the layers of steel plates on top of each others, where the decks have collapsed. The Manacles are very tidal, which means life is abundant. The wreck has a covering of pink sea fans, as well as dead mans fingers and various sea weeds. Cup corals, jewel anemones, Nudibranchs, as well as a wide range of fish are normally encountered. A wreck dive worth doing several times, even then you probably still wouldn't see the whole wreck. Most dives start around the boilers, from there you have a lot of choices. Quite a few divers spend most of the dive around the boilers, which can take a whole dive to investigate, some will head off towards the stern or to the bow.

Whatever you do, take your time, you won't see it all in one dive. Maximum depth is around 28m at high water, if you remain on the wreckage, you can get greater depth just off the wreck towards the north or north east. The top of the boilers is around 14m at low water. Most of the wreckage is around 20-22m.

The Mohegan's boilers

The next most visited wreck, is the Spyridion Vagliano, a Greek freighter that sank in 1888. It is now well broken and spread around in a general depth of about 15m.

The remains of the Spyridion Vagliano's boiler

An interesting dive in itself but we are on the Manacles, where we have the Mohegan and numerous reefs. The Andola is a pleasant enough dive too, it is also quite shallow, nestled close into the rocks in just a few metres of water, it can be sheltered from most wind directions, apart from the dreaded easterly or southerlies. It is also a lot less tidal than the rest of the Manacles. Other wrecks in the area that are occasionally dived are the Lady Dalhousie and the HMS Primrose.

Life, that is what the Manacles reef system is really famous for. Whether it is commercial or recreational fishermen after a good days catch, or, rare species that can only be spotted by divers. The Manacles has it all. So much in fact, that it is now a Marine Conservation Zone. It is mainly protected for the Pink Sea Fan Anemone and the Rock Lobster (Crawfish). The Rock Lobster has been in a major decline for decades, whereas the

Pink Sea Fan Anemone is a very rare creature indeed. Since 2015 though, Rock Lobsters have been spotted on many dives around the Manacles and Falmouth Bay. More Rock Lobsters are being spotted in the area than the common lobster.

All of the most commonly dived pinnacles are covered in Jewel Anemones, of all colours. There is also an abundance of Plumose Anemones, Dead Mans Fingers and Pink Sea Fans. Fish are also quite plentiful, Wrasse are always spotted close to the rocks, farther away you can find schooling Bass and Mackerel. The Manacles are also a good place to find Nudibranchs. Most of this life is around the steeply sided pinnacles of Raglan's Reef, Pen Wyn and Vase Rock. Pen Wyn is also the final resting place of the Mohegan's rudder. Carn Du is rarely dived but it is worth diving for a change from the other pinnacles. The shallow wrecks are usually covered in kelp throughout the year, quite a lot of it dies off during the winter months but soon grows back as the days lengthen. A world class dive site with something for everyone.

Jewel Anemones on Raglans Reef

Most dives on the Manacles are completed at slack water. During big spring tides, slack water can be very short, shelter can be found behind some of the pinnacles. During small neap tides, most sites are dive-able at all times. If you are taking your own boat to the Manacles, do not anchor the boat, if the current does start to run, it can be very difficult to bring the anchor up. Also, any divers would be drifting away quite quickly, especially on a spring tide.

The Manacles reef system still holds many secrets. There are two known wrecks yet to be found. There have been some items found but of ages unrelated to the known wrecks, they are signs of other wrecks that are as of yet unknown. There is a lone three stage steam engine lying in a gully near Maen Voes, a few miles away, just off Porthoustock, there is a lone ship's boiler. These may never be identified, they may be clues to further wrecks, they may be related, it is hard to tell.

Within the newspaper archives, there are stories of many wrecks on the Manacles, many of which have never been found. Yet.

For the diver, Falmouth has almost everything they could want. Whether they are looking for wrecks, reefs, rocks, wildlife, food or deep technical diving, Falmouth has it all.

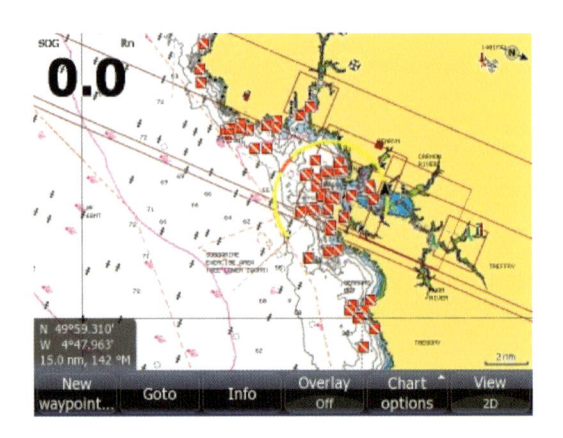

Some of the dive sites on the authors chart plotter.

The above screen grab is rotated to show as much of the area as possible, the north direction is indicated in the top right of the image. The beige area is land, the blue is shallow water i.e. less than 10m, the white is deeper water. The red squares with white stripes are the regular dive sites. The wrecks symbols dotted around the white areas, are deeper wrecks, there are a lot of them.

The author taking the obligatory selfie.

Glossary

Within this guide, there are terms which divers and fishermen will understand. For those that don't, here is a little help:

Carrick Roads - The main estuary at Falmouth, where the river Fal, the Percuil river, Penryn river as well as three other rivers meet.

CCR Rebreather - A unit that re-circulates the breathing gases, allowing for increased times at depth.

Drift or Drifting - What happens to a diver when caught in a current, the diver uses the current to cover the sea bed.

Marine Conservation Zone (MCZ) - An area protected for either it's diversity of marine life or for specific species.

Neap Tides - Smallest change in tide height between high and low water.

Nudibranch - A sea slug, usually very colourful.

S.S. - Steam Ship (s.s.)

S.V. - Sailing Vessel (s.v.)

Side Scan Sonar - An enhanced version of a traditional sonar, creating 3D looking images of the underwater world.

Slack Water - A period when the tide stops before changing direction, for Falmouth area this is roughly one hour after high or low tide at Falmouth.

Spring Tides - Largest change in tide height between high and low water.

Technical Diving - Diving that includes any planned decompression, where planned stops have to be made to avoid the bends.

Trimix - A mixture of oxygen, nitrogen and helium. Used as a breathing gas to allow divers to dive safely beyond recreational and sport diving limits.

Bibliography

Shipwrecks of the British Isles Volume 1 - Richard and Bridget Larn

Wreck and Rescue round the Cornish coast, III, the story of the south coast lifeboats - Noall & Farr

www.wrecksite.eu

Further Reading

Beneath Cornish Seas - Mark Webster

Great British Marine Animals - Paul Naylor

100 Best Dives in Cornwall - Charles Hood

Dive South Cornwall - Richard Larn

Falmouth town and part of Falmouth Bay.